I0490381

JAPAN BOUND: YOUR ULTIMATE GUIDE TO SECURING A WORK VISA AND NAILING JOB INTERVIEWS

BY

Brian Takahashi

© Copyright 2023 by Brian Takahashi - All rights reserved.

It is not legal to reproduce, duplicate, or transmit any part of this document electronically or in print. Recording of this publication is strictly prohibited.

TABLE OF CONTENTS

Introduction

Are you interested in working in Japan? Japan is an exciting and dynamic country with a rich culture and fascinating history. Many dreams of working and living in Japan, but navigating the visa requirements and application process can be daunting. That's where this guide comes in.

This book will provide a comprehensive overview of the visa requirements and application process for working in Japan. We will also guide you through the various types of work visas, the eligibility criteria for each class, and the duration of stay and renewal options available.

We will then delve into the job search process in Japan, including an overview of job search resources, resume and cover letter tips, networking strategies, and standard job interview questions.

Finally, we will provide you with a step-by-step guide on how to apply for a Japanese work visa, including preparing the necessary documents, completing the visa application form, submitting the application and paying the fees, and tracking the status of your application.

Whether you are a recent graduate, a seasoned professional, or simply interested in exploring Japan's opportunities, this guide will be your essential companion on your journey toward warding and living in Japan.

PART I: Why Work in Japan?

Working in Japan can be a gratifying experience for foreigners seeking to explore a new culture and advance their careers. With a robust economy and dynamic business culture, Japan offers many opportunities for foreign workers.

One of the primary advantages of working in Japan is the pervasive professionalism and dedication to quality that permeates the country's business community. From small startups to large multinational corporations, Japanese companies are renowned for their commitment to excellence and prioritize employee training and development.

In addition to its strong work ethic, Japan is famous for its rich cultural heritage and deep appreciation for tradition. As a foreign worker in Japan, you will have the chance to immerse yourself in the country's unique customs and practices and explore its fascinating history.

However, working in Japan as a foreigner can also pose some challenges. For example, language barriers can be a significant obstacle for those who need to be fluent in Japanese. Nonetheless, many Japanese companies recognize the value foreign workers bring to their organizations and frequently offer language support and other resources to help them succeed.

Another challenge foreign workers may encounter adjusting to the cultural differences between Japan and their home country. Nevertheless, with an open mind and a willingness to learn, most foreign workers can adapt quickly and thrive in Japan's dynamic business culture.

Whether you aspire to advance your career, explore a new culture, or broaden your horizons, Japan provides many opportunities for those willing to embrace its distinctive challenges and rewards.

Chapter One: The Land of Opportunity and Why Working in Japan is a Great Career Move

High standard of living:

Japan is known for its high living standard, which results from several factors. First and foremost, Japan has a highly educated and skilled workforce. The country strongly emphasizes education, and the Japanese education system is known for its rigor and high academic standards. This has helped to develop a highly skilled workforce with strong technical and problem-solving abilities, which has, in turn, helped to drive Japan's economic success. Many people who work in Japan enjoy a high quality of life and have access to many amenities and services that are not available in other countries.

In addition to a skilled workforce, Japan has a strong economy built on innovation and technological advancement. The country is home to many leading technology and manufacturing companies and has been at the forefront of robotics, electronics, and automotive engineering developments. This has helped to drive economic growth and create high-paying jobs for many Japanese workers.

The social welfare system provides support to those in need. The country has universal healthcare coverage, a comprehensive social security system, and a range of other programs designed to help people in need. This has helped to reduce poverty and improve the quality of life for many Japanese citizens.

A robust infrastructure is another factor contributing to its high standard of living. The country has a modern and efficient transportation system, including a high-speed rail network that connects cities across the country. The government also has a well-developed energy infrastructure, with a mix of renewable and non-renewable sources that help ensure a reliable energy supply.

A culture of social responsibility and community engagement are significant parts of Japanese life. The country strongly emphasizes social harmony and community building, and many Japanese citizens are actively involved in community organizations and volunteer groups. This helps to create a strong sense of social cohesion and contributes to a high quality of life for many people in Japan.

Japan's high standard of living results from a combination of factors, including a highly skilled workforce, a strong economy, a comprehensive social welfare system, modern infrastructure, and a culture of social responsibility and community engagement. These factors have helped create a prosperous and thriving society that is highly regarded worldwide.

Strong economy:

Japan is a significant player in the global economy, with a GDP of over $5 trillion and numerous multinational corporations. This makes it an attractive destination for skilled workers, especially in technology, engineering, finance, and education.

One reason for Japan's success is its highly educated and skilled workforce. The country strongly emphasizes education, with a rigorous education system that instills high academic standards. As a result, Japan has developed a highly skilled workforce with strong technical and problem-solving abilities, which has helped drive its economic success.

Another factor is Japan's robust manufacturing sector, built on technological innovation and advanced production techniques. The country is home to many leading automotive, electronics, and machinery manufacturing companies, and these companies have been pioneers in technological innovation and have contributed significantly to Japan's economic growth.

Japan also has a strong culture of innovation and entrepreneurship. The country has created a supportive environment for startups and entrepreneurs, with numerous policies and programs encouraging innovation and entrepreneurship. This has led to the development of a thriving startup ecosystem in Japan that has significantly contributed to the country's economic growth.

Infrastructure is another area where Japan excels. The country has a modern and efficient transportation system, including a high-speed rail network that connects cities across the country. It also has a well-developed infrastructure that ensures a reliable energy supply from renewable and non-renewable sources.

Japan's highly developed financial system is also essential to its economic success. The country has a well-regulated and stable financial system, with a strong network of banks and other financial institutions that provide funding and support for businesses.

A supportive government has played a crucial role in driving economic growth. The government has developed a range of policies and programs designed to support businesses, encourage innovation, and create jobs. This has helped to create a favorable environment for economic growth and development in Japan.

Japan's strong economy results from a combination of factors: a highly skilled workforce, a strong manufacturing sector, a culture of innovation and entrepreneurship, modern infrastructure, a developed financial system, and a supportive government. These factors have helped create a thriving economy that is highly regarded worldwide.

Cultural Experience:

Japan has a rich and fascinating culture that many people are eager to experience firsthand. Working in Japan allows one to immerse oneself in Japanese culture, learn the language, and explore the country's unique customs and traditions.

Understanding Japan's culture can help individuals develop stronger relationships with Japanese colleagues and clients and communicate more effectively with them. This can lead to better collaboration, more effective problem-solving, and substantial business outcomes.

Having experience with Japanese culture can help individuals to develop strong cross-cultural communication skills, which can be highly valuable in today's globalized business environment. This includes understanding different communication styles, social norms, and business etiquette in Japan.

Japan has a highly hierarchical society, and individuals with experience with Japanese culture understand the importance of respecting senior colleagues and clients. This can help build trust and credibility and lead to more significant opportunities for career advancement.

Individuals with Japanese cultural experience understand the importance of hard work, dedication, and attention to detail. Japan is known for its attention to detail, which can be highly valuable in many industries, including manufacturing, engineering, and technology.

Japan has a unique culture that is different from many Western countries, and individuals who have experience with Japanese culture are often highly adaptable and can easily navigate different cultural contexts. This can be highly valuable in today's globalized business environment, where cross-cultural communication and collaboration are increasingly important.

Having experience with Japanese culture can be highly beneficial for career success, providing individuals with a range of valuable skills and perspectives that can help them to excel in the workplace.

Networking Opportunities:

Japan is home to many international organizations and professional associations, which provide excellent networking opportunities for foreign workers. These connections can be valuable for building relationships, finding job opportunities, and advancing one's career. In Japan, building and maintaining relationships is highly valued, known as "Kizuna," or bonds of friendship, and it is seen as a critical aspect of doing business. Building solid relationships with other professionals can lead to new job opportunities, recommendations, and business partnerships. Additionally, having a reliable network can provide access to information and resources that may not be available otherwise.

Japan has a group-oriented culture where people are encouraged to work together and support each other. This extends to the business world, where people often work in teams to achieve common goals. Building a solid professional network allows individuals to tap into this collaborative spirit, making it easier to work with others and accomplish shared objectives. Furthermore, the seniority-based system in Japan is still prevalent, where individuals are valued based on their age and years of experience. A solid network can be particularly beneficial for younger professionals just starting their careers, as it allows them to learn from more experienced colleagues and gain insights into the industry.

Japan is also known for its high-trust culture, where relationships are built on trust and mutual respect. By making a solid professional network, individuals can demonstrate their trustworthiness and reliability to others in their field, leading to new opportunities and increased concern within the industry. In Japan, face-to-face communication is highly valued, and many business deals are still conducted in person. Building a solid professional network allows individuals to meet others in their field and establish personal connections, which can lead to new opportunities and collaborations.

Professional networking in Japan can advance one's career due to the importance of relationships, group-oriented culture, seniority-based system, trust-based culture, and the extent of face-to-face communication. By building strong work relationships, individuals can tap into these cultural values and gain access to new opportunities, information, and resources.

Generous Employee Benefits:

Working in Japan can be an attractive option for foreign workers due to the generous employee benefits provided by Japanese companies, such as health insurance, paid vacation time, and bonuses. These benefits reflect the cultural norms, government policies, historical developments, and competition for talent in Japan.

Japan is a collectivist society that values group harmony and the well-being of the collective. Companies in Japan tend to view their employees as part of a more prominent family, leading to a strong sense of obligation to take care of employees. Companies' generous employee benefits, such as paid time off, bonuses, and health insurance, reflect this cultural norm.

The Japanese government has implemented various policies to encourage companies to provide generous employee benefits, including the Employment Insurance System, which requires all companies to offer health insurance, pension plans, and workers' compensation. Companies that provide different benefits beyond the law's requirements can also receive tax incentives.

Japan's post-World War II economic miracle led to the creation of the lifetime employment system, which provided job security and long-term career prospects to employees in return for their loyalty and dedication. This system led to the development of a culture of mutual support between companies and employees, which is reflected in the generous employee benefits provided by companies.

As the Japanese economy has become more competitive, companies have realized the importance of attracting and retaining top talent. Providing generous employee benefits is one way to differentiate themselves and attract the best. This talent competition has led to an increase in the overall level of benefits provided by companies.

Their generous employee benefits system is due to cultural norms emphasizing group harmony, government policies encouraging companies to provide benefits, and historical developments creating a culture of mutual support and competition for talent. This system benefits employees and companies, promoting job security, well-being, and productivity.

Chapter Two: Overcoming Obstacles and the Challenges of Working in Japan

Language Barrier:

Many foreign workers may need help to overcome the language barrier when working in Japan. Japanese is relatively easy to learn and can pose communication and language barriers in the workplace, hindering one's ability to form relationships with colleagues and clients and impeding career advancement.

One of the primary challenges in learning Japanese is the complexity of the writing system, which uses three different scripts: kanji (Chinese characters), hiragana, and katakana. Reading and writing thousands of kanji characters can take years of study and practice. Moreover, Japanese uses many homophones, making it challenging for learners to distinguish between words in conversation.

Another significant challenge for foreign workers is the grammar and syntax of Japanese. The subject-object-verb (SOV) word order in Japanese is the opposite of the subject-verb-object (SVO) word order in English. This can make it challenging for learners to form sentences that sound natural to Japanese speakers.

The complex honorific system in Japan is another challenge for foreign workers. The honorific system shows respect and politeness in different social situations. It includes various verb forms, sentence structures, and vocabulary choices depending on the social status of the speaker and listener. This can be particularly difficult for learners from cultures emphasizing hierarchy and formality less.

Finally, limited opportunities for practice outside of Japan can make it challenging for learners to develop fluency in Japanese. Unlike English, which is widely spoken worldwide and has many resources available for learners, Japanese is primarily spoken in Japan and Japanese communities abroad.

Despite these challenges, with dedication and consistent effort, foreign workers can achieve fluency in Japanese and succeed in a Japanese-speaking work environment. Language learning is crucial for overcoming communication barriers and building relationships with colleagues and clients. It may take years of practice, but the rewards of mastering Japanese can be significant for one's career advancement and personal growth.

Cultural Differences:

Japanese culture is rich and unique and can be difficult for foreigners to navigate. Several cultural differences can be challenging for foreign workers, including the emphasis on group harmony over individual achievement, the strict hierarchical structure of many workplaces, and the expectation of long working hours.

First, Japan is an island nation that has been relatively isolated from the rest of the world for much of its history. This isolation, combined with Japan's unique geography and natural resources, has contributed to developing a distinct culture different from neighboring countries.

Second, Japan has a long and rich history that various cultural and religious influences, including Buddhism, Confucianism, and Shintoism, have shaped. These influences have profoundly impacted Japanese values and customs, such as the emphasis on respect for authority, group harmony, and the importance of nature.

Third, Japan has a collectivist culture that strongly emphasizes the needs and interests of the group over the individual. This contrasts with many Western cultures, which emphasize individualism and personal achievement. This collectivist culture is reflected in many aspects of Japanese society, including the strict hierarchical structure of many workplaces and the focus on consensus-based decision-making.

Fourth, Japan's unique aesthetic tradition values simplicity, elegance, and attention to detail. This aesthetic is reflected in many aspects of Japanese culture, including art, architecture, and even food presentation.

Fifth, Japan has a unique approach to social etiquette that can be challenging for foreigners to navigate. This includes complex honorific language, bowing as a form of greeting, and strict rules around gift-giving and business card exchange.

The historical, social, and cultural factors that have shaped Japanese culture have contributed to its unique and distinctive character. While these cultural differences can pose challenges for foreign workers, they can also provide opportunities for personal growth, cross-cultural exchange, and new perspectives on the world.

High Cost of Living:

Japan is a country known for its high standard of living, with excellent public services such as healthcare, transportation, and education. However, this comes at a cost, as Japan is also an expensive country to live in, particularly in major cities like Tokyo and Osaka. Rent, transportation, and food costs can be significantly higher than in other countries, challenging some foreign workers, particularly those with lower-paying jobs.

The cost of providing these excellent public services is high, which leads to a higher cost of living. Additionally, Japanese consumers tend to demand high-quality products and services, which drives up prices. This emphasis on quality and craftsmanship is a cultural norm in Japan that contributes to the high cost of living. Japanese consumers also tend to place a high value on convenience, which can lead to higher prices for goods and services that offer comfort.

The Japanese government has implemented various policies contributing to the high living cost. For example, increased taxes on imports and strict regulations on foreign goods and services make imported products more expensive. Additionally, Japan's complex distribution system and strict rules on businesses can make it difficult for foreign companies to compete, leading to higher prices.

Japan is a small island nation with limited natural resources, making producing goods and services domestically difficult. As a result, Japan relies heavily on imports, which can be expensive due to high transportation costs and import taxes. Furthermore, Japan's aging population strains the economy and contributes to the high cost of living. As the population ages, there is a greater demand for healthcare, social services, and other support systems, which are expensive to provide.

The high cost of living can be attributed to various factors, including the high standard of living, government policies that make imported products more expensive, cultural norms that place a premium on quality and convenience, limited resources, and an aging population. Despite these challenges, Japan remains a desirable place to live and work due to its excellent public services, high quality of life, and a strong economy.

Limited Career Advancement:

Japan's work culture is known for being highly structured and hierarchical, with a focus on traditional values and conformity. While these elements can appeal to some, they can also create obstacles for foreign workers looking to advance in their careers. One of the most significant challenges facing foreign workers in Japan is limited career advancement opportunities.

Many Japanese companies have a strict hierarchical structure that can make it difficult for foreign workers to advance. Additionally, there may be a preference for hiring Japanese workers over foreigners, particularly in specific industries. In Japan, promotions and job opportunities are often based on seniority rather than merit or performance. This means that employees must wait their turn to move up the corporate ladder, which can be frustrating for younger or more ambitious workers.

Companies often have a highly traditional corporate culture, which values loyalty and conformity over the individual initiative and risk-taking. This can make it difficult for employees with different ideas or approaches to succeed in the corporate world. Furthermore, the Japanese education system is highly structured and emphasizes rote learning and conformity. This can lead to a highly skilled workforce that needs more creativity and innovation, making it difficult for employees to stand out and advance in their careers.

Another challenge for employees in Japan is the need for job mobility. Employees are often expected to stay with the same company for their entire career, making gaining new experiences and skills necessary for career advancement difficult. In addition, networking is essential to career advancement in many countries. Still, in Japan, the hierarchical corporate culture can make it difficult for employees to build relationships with senior executives or influential people in their industry.

Gender and age discrimination are also prevalent in Japan, with women and older workers facing challenges in terms of career advancement opportunities. This can limit their career prospects and make it difficult for them to advance in their chosen field.

Japan's highly structured and hierarchical corporate culture, seniority-based system, traditional values, education system, lack of job mobility, limited networking opportunities, and discrimination can all contribute to limited career advancement opportunities for employees. While there are efforts underway to change this culture, progress has been slow, and it remains a challenge for many workers in Japan.

Work Culture:

Japan's work culture is often described as demanding and intense, with extended hours and a strong emphasis on loyalty and dedication to one's employer. This can challenge foreign workers who are used to a more relaxed or flexible work environment. The roots of Japan's work culture can be traced back to historical and cultural factors, such as the country's long-standing value of hard work and dedication to one's company or organization. The education system reinforces this cultural value, emphasizing discipline, diligence, and conformity.

A strong work ethic and an emphasis on productivity partly fueled Japan's post-World War II economic growth. This led to a corporate culture that valued long hours and sacrifices for the company's good. Japan's seniority-based system also contributes to a culture of overwork. Employees are expected to demonstrate loyalty and commitment to the company by working long hours and putting in extra effort.

In Japan, job mobility is often limited, with employees expected to stay with the same company for their careers. This can create a sense of obligation and loyalty to the company, as employees feel they must work hard and sacrifice their personal lives to advance in their careers. Additionally, Japan's social safety net is relatively limited compared to other developed countries, which can pressure employees to work long hours to provide for themselves and their families.

Japan's aging population and declining birth rate have pressured the workforce to be more productive and efficient. This has led to a culture of overwork, as companies need help to maintain their productivity levels with a shrinking force. Efforts are underway to address these issues, such as promoting work-life balance and reducing long working hours. However, progress has been slow, and it remains a challenge for many workers in Japan to balance their work and personal lives.

Discrimination:

Discrimination against foreign workers is a significant problem in Japan, and it can affect their job prospects, work conditions, and overall well-being. Foreign workers may face discrimination during hiring, limiting their opportunities in specific industries, such as finance, law, and government. This can make it difficult for foreign workers to find employment in their field and may force them to accept lower-paying jobs outside their expertise.

Even when foreign workers are hired, they may face discrimination in the workplace. They may be excluded from important meetings or decision-making processes and may receive a different level of training or opportunities for advancement than Japanese workers. Foreign workers may also experience unequal pay and longer working hours than their Japanese counterparts, creating a sense of inequality and injustice.

In addition, foreign workers in Japan may face discrimination in their daily lives. They may encounter racial slurs or harassment and have difficulty finding housing or accessing public services. Such experiences can create a sense of isolation and alienation, which can affect their mental health and overall well-being.

Another issue for foreign workers in Japan is the language barrier. While Japan is known for its high level of English education, many Japanese workers may need to be fluent in English. This can create a communication gap between Japanese and foreign workers, leading to misunderstandings and conflicts in the workplace.

Gender discrimination is also a problem for foreign workers in Japan, with women experiencing a double burden of discrimination based on their gender and nationality. They may be subject to sexual harassment or discrimination based on traditional gender roles. They may find it challenging to secure employment in specific industries because they prefer male workers.

Discrimination against foreign workers in Japan is a complex issue that affects their job prospects, work conditions, and overall well-being. It requires the joint effort of employers, government officials, and society to address this issue and create a more inclusive and welcoming environment for foreign workers in Japan. By addressing these challenges, Japan can tap into the full potential of its foreign workforce and benefit from a more diverse and multicultural society.

PART II: Navigating the Job Market and Visa Process in Japan

Japan is known for its rich culture, advanced technology, and strong economy. With over 126 million people, Japan's diverse and dynamic workforce attracts professionals worldwide. Whether you are a recent graduate, a seasoned professional, or an entrepreneur looking to start a business in Japan, various opportunities are available.

However, to fully take advantage of these opportunities, it is vital to have a thorough understanding of the visa system, job market, and business culture in Japan. This section aims to provide a comprehensive guide to these critical aspects of living and working in Japan.

The first part of this section will focus on visas and eligibility criteria. Japan has several types of visas available for foreigners, each with its requirements and limitations. We will provide an overview of the most common types of visas, including work visas, student visas, and permanent resident visas. We will also discuss the eligibility criteria for each type of visa, including age, education, language proficiency, financial stability, and criminal record.

Next, we will delve into the job market in Japan. Japan is home to some of the world's largest and most successful corporations, including Toyota, Sony, and Mitsubishi. These companies offer various employment opportunities, from entry-level to senior executive roles. We will explore the job search process in Japan, including how to find job openings, apply for jobs, and prepare for interviews.

Finally, we will discuss the business culture in Japan. Japan has a unique and complex business culture with its customs and etiquette. Understanding and adhering to these customs is crucial for success in the Japanese business world. We will cover business dress codes, gift-giving, and communication styles.

By the end of this section, readers will have a solid understanding of Japan's visa system, job market, and business culture. Whether you plan to study, work, or start a business in Japan, this section will provide the information you need to succeed in this dynamic and exciting country.

Chapter Three: Navigating Japanese Visas with A Comprehensive Guide to Requirements and Eligibility

Short-term Stay Visa:

In Japan, a short-term stay visa allows foreigners to enter and stay in the country for a limited period, typically up to 90 days. This type of visa is intended for individuals who wish to visit Japan for a short period for various purposes, such as tourism, business, or attending conferences.

To apply for a short-term stay visa, applicants must provide certain documents, including a valid passport, a completed visa application form, and supporting documents such as an itinerary of their trip, a letter of invitation from a Japanese company or organization, and proof of financial stability. In some cases, applicants may also need to provide a certificate of employment or a reference letter.

One crucial factor to note is that holders of short-term stay visas are not allowed to work in Japan during their stay. However, they can engage in certain activities such as attending conferences, conducting market research, or participating in cultural events.

Short-term stay visas can be obtained at Japanese embassies or consulates in the applicant's home country or country of residence. The visa application process can take several weeks, so it is recommended that applicants apply well in advance of their planned trip.

It is important to note that short-term stay visas are distinct from other types of visas, such as work visas, student visas, and permanent resident visas. These visas have different requirements and allow for extended stays and various activities.

The short-term stay visa in Japan allows foreigners to enter and stay in Japan for a limited period, typically up to 90 days, for purposes such as tourism or business. Applicants must provide certain documents and are not allowed to work in Japan during their stay.

Cultural Activities Visa:

The Cultural Activities visa in Japan is a unique opportunity for individuals seeking to participate in traditional Japanese arts, music, dance, or language studies. It is intended for those who avoid full-time work or business activities. Applicants must provide detailed information about their planned cultural activities to be eligible for this visa, such as their stay's duration, location, and purpose. Additionally, applicants must demonstrate their qualifications or experience in the relevant field and prove they have sufficient financial means to support themselves during their stay in Japan.

The duration of the Cultural Activities visa depends on the length of the cultural activity or program, and it can range from several months to one year. Holders of this visa must refrain from engaging in activities outside the scope of their designated cultural activities, such as working full-time or engaging in business activities. To apply for this visa, applicants must submit their application at a Japanese embassy or consulate in their home country or country of residence, along with a valid passport, a completed visa application form, a recent photograph, and any additional documents required by the embassy or consulate.

To be eligible for a Cultural Activities Visa in Japan, applicants must meet the following requirements: the purpose of their stay must be to engage in cultural activities, they must have a sponsor in Japan who can provide a letter of invitation and support their cultural activities, they must have the necessary qualifications and expertise to engage in the cultural activities they plan to pursue, they must have sufficient funds to support themselves during their stay in Japan, and they must be in good health and have no criminal record.

It is essential to note that the Cultural Activities Visa is intended for someone other than those who wish to work in Japan or pursue long-term study. Those who want to work or study in Japan must apply for the appropriate visa type. Additionally, the application process for a Cultural Activities Visa can be quite complex. It is recommended that applicants seek the assistance of a sponsor or immigration lawyer to ensure that all requirements are met and the application is submitted correctly.

The Cultural Activities visa is an excellent opportunity for individuals who want to immerse themselves in Japanese culture and gain valuable experience in their field of interest. It is crucial to read and meet the eligibility requirements carefully and understand the limitations of the visa, as it is intended for cultural activities only and not for full-time work or business activities. With proper preparation and support, applicants can successfully apply and enjoy their time exploring Japan's rich cultural heritage.

Working Visa:

A working visa is granted to foreign nationals who have received a job offer from a Japanese employer and is valid for up to 5 years. Let's examine the various requirements for obtaining a working visa in Japan.

Firstly, an individual must have a job offer from a Japanese employer to apply for a work visa. The employer must apply for a Certificate of Eligibility (COE) on behalf of the employee. Additionally, the individual must have the necessary education or experience for the job. This can include specific degrees or certifications depending on the type of work visa being applied for. For example, a Skilled Labor visa may only require a high school diploma and relevant work experience. In contrast, a Specialist in Humanities/International Services visa may require a bachelor's degree or higher in a specific field.

Moreover, the individual must have a clean criminal record and be in good standing with the law, and a background check may be required to prove this. The individual must also have a valid passport that will not expire for at least six months and meet the health requirements set by the Japanese government, which may include a medical examination and vaccinations. Additionally, the individual must have sufficient funds to support themselves in Japan until they receive their first paycheck. The exact amount required can vary depending on the type of work visa, but generally, it is recommended to have at least 200,000 yen (around $1,800) in savings.

Some jobs may require the individual to have a certain level of proficiency in Japanese. However, not all work visas have language requirements. It's important to note that specific eligibility criteria also exist for each type of work visa. For instance, an Engineer/Specialist in Humanities/International Services visa is for individuals with particular skills and expertise in fields such as engineering, science, humanities, or international services. The individual must have a degree or equivalent experience in the relevant field to be eligible. On the other hand, a Skilled Labor visa is for individuals with skills and expertise in industries such as construction, manufacturing, or agriculture. To be eligible, the individual must have a certain level of knowledge in the relevant sector.

Each type of work visa in Japan has its own set of requirements and eligibility criteria. Therefore, it is essential to carefully review the details of the specific type of work visa being applied for.

Working Holiday Visa:

A working holiday visa is a unique opportunity for young people to experience life and work in a foreign country for a designated period. In Japan, this visa is known as the "Working Holiday Visa," It is available to citizens of select countries between the ages of 18 and 30 (or 35 for some countries) and who wish to stay in Japan for up to one year.

To be eligible in Japan, applicants must meet several requirements, including having a valid passport from an eligible country, being a resident of the country where they apply for the visa, having a certain amount of money in savings, being in good health, and not having a criminal record. The visa is intended for people who want to supplement their travel funds with short-term work rather than those who want to work full-time or live in Japan permanently.

Once approved, this visa allows holders to work in various fields, such as hospitality, tourism, retail, and agriculture. However, it is essential to note that the visa is not intended for jobs that require professional qualifications, such as doctors or lawyers. The visa allows a unique experience to immerse oneself in Japanese culture and gain valuable work experience while exploring the country.

Applicants must provide a detailed itinerary of their travel plans and proof of their return ticket or sufficient funds to purchase one. It is important to note that the eligibility criteria for a working holiday visa may be subject to change, and applicants should check the latest requirements before applying. Additionally, the number of working holiday visas issued yearly is limited, and the application process can be competitive.

It is an excellent opportunity for young people to work and travel in Japan for up to one year. It is a unique way to immerse oneself in Japanese culture and gain valuable work experience while exploring the country. However, applicants must meet specific eligibility requirements and carefully read and understand the limitations of the visa. They should be aware that the number of working holiday visas issued each year is limited.

Student Visa:

A student visa in Japan is issued to foreign nationals accepted to study at a Japanese educational institution. The visa is valid for the course of study, and students can work part-time (up to 28 hours per week) to support themselves. To apply for a student visa, you must be enrolled in Japanese educational institution such as a language school, vocational school, college, or university.

In addition to enrollment, several other requirements must be met to obtain a student visa. Firstly, you must provide proof of financial support, such as bank statements, to show that you can cover living costs and study in Japan. Secondly, you must have a valid passport that does not expire for at least six months after your intended stay in Japan. You must also provide an admission letter or certificate of enrollment from your educational institution in Japan, fill out and submit a visa application form, and provide a recent passport-sized photo of yourself. Depending on your home country and the duration of your stay in Japan, you may need to provide a health certificate and demonstrate your proficiency in the Japanese language.

To be eligible for a student visa in Japan, the educational institution you attend must be accredited by the Japanese government. You must also have sufficient funds to cover the costs of living and studying in Japan, not have a criminal record in your home country or Japan, have a clear intent to return to your home country after completing your studies in Japan, be in good health, and have the academic ability to succeed in your chosen course of study.

It is important to note that the specific requirements and eligibility criteria for a Japanese student visa may vary depending on your home country and the educational institution you are attending. Therefore, you should check with your home country's Japanese embassy or consulate for the most up-to-date and accurate information.

Dependant Visa:

A dependent visa in Japan is designed for the family members of foreign nationals who hold a valid work or student visa in Japan. The dependent visa allows the family members to stay in Japan with the visa holder for their stay.

To qualify for a dependent visa in Japan, specific eligibility requirements must be met:

Relationship with the visa holder: The dependent must be the spouse or child of the visa holder. In some cases, parents or siblings may also be eligible.

Financial support: The visa holder must be able to provide financial support to the dependent during their stay in Japan.

Proof of relationship: The dependent must provide evidence of their relationship with the visa holder, such as a marriage or birth certificate.

Valid passport: The dependent must have a valid passport.

Health and character requirements: The dependent must meet the health and character requirements set by the Japanese government.

To apply for a dependent visa in Japan, the following requirements must be fulfilled:

Application form: The dependent must complete and submit a dependent visa application form.

Passport: The dependent must have a valid passport.

Photo: The dependent must provide a recent passport-sized photograph.

Certificate of eligibility: The visa holder must apply for a Certificate of Eligibility (COE) on behalf of the dependent. This certificate confirms that the dependent meets the requirements for a dependent visa.

Proof of relationship: The dependent must provide evidence of their relationship with the visa holder, such as a marriage or birth certificate.

Financial documents: The visa holder must provide proof of their financial ability to support the dependent during their stay in Japan, such as bank statements or employment contracts.

Health certificate: The dependent may need to provide a health certificate if required by the Japanese government.

Overall, the dependent visa in Japan allows family members of foreign nationals to stay together during their time in Japan. The visa holder must meet specific eligibility requirements and provide financial support to the dependent. In contrast, the dependent must provide proof of their relationship with the visa holder and meet the health and character requirements set by the Japanese government.

Trainee Visa:

The trainee visa is issued to foreign nationals who wish to participate in a trainee program in Japan. The program is designed to provide technical and vocational training to foreigners and is typically sponsored by Japanese companies. The visa is valid for up to one year.

Eligibility for the trainee visa is based on the individual's desire to learn a specific skill or trade, such as language, technology, or culture. It is typically for individuals who do not have a bachelor's degree, as other types of visas may be more appropriate for those with higher levels of education. Additionally, the individual must have a sponsor in Japan who is willing to provide them with training and support during their stay. This sponsor could be a company, organization, or educational institution registered with the Japanese government to accept trainees.

A valid contract between the trainee and their sponsor outlining the details of the training program, including the duration, content, and compensation, is required. Trainees must also have a basic understanding of the Japanese language to communicate with their sponsor and colleagues. However, proficiency requirements may vary depending on the type of training and the sponsor.

Trainees must be in good health and have a medical examination before coming to Japan. They may also need to provide evidence of certain vaccinations. Additionally, trainees must have sufficient financial support to cover their living expenses while in Japan, as they may only be permitted to work in their training program. Trainees must be at least 18 and under 30 years old at the time of application.

It is important to note that trainee visas have been scrutinized in recent years due to reports of exploitation and abuse of trainees by their sponsors. As a result, the Japanese government has implemented stricter regulations and oversight to prevent such violations from occurring.

Technical Internship Visa:

The Technical Internship Visa is issued to foreign nationals who wish to participate in a technical internship program in Japan. The program is intended to provide specialized training to foreigners, and Japanese companies typically sponsor it. The visa is valid for up to five years.

Applicants must meet specific eligibility criteria to apply for the Technical Internship Visa. Firstly, applicants must be between the ages of 18 and 39. Secondly, they must have a valid passport and be citizens of a country participating in the Technical Intern Training Program. Lastly, applicants must have completed at least 12 years of education or have work experience in a field related to the training they will receive in Japan.

The application process for the Technical Internship Visa involves finding a sending organization that the Japanese government approves to send trainees to Japan. The sending organization will assist with the application process and support the trainee's stay in Japan. After finding a sending organization, the applicant must provide documents such as a passport, a certificate of education or work experience, and a certificate of Japanese language proficiency (depending on the type of training they will receive). The sending organization will then submit the application to the Japanese government on the trainee's behalf.

Trainees can stay in Japan for up to five years, depending on the type of training they will receive. The training will be provided by a hosting company, providing the trainee with room and board. Trainees will receive a monthly allowance for living expenses, which will vary depending on the type of training and the region of Japan they will be staying in. Trainees are required to attend Japanese language classes and pass a proficiency test.

Trainees are only allowed to work in the specific field they were trained in. They are not allowed to work overtime or on holidays, and their working hours must be at most eight hours per day. The host company must provide a safe working environment and ensure that trainees receive appropriate training and supervision.

It is important to note that the Technical Intern Training Program has faced criticism for allowing companies to exploit trainees and not providing adequate protections for their rights and safety. The Japanese government has tried to improve the program and strengthen protections for trainees, but it remains a controversial issue.

Permanent Resident Visa:

The Permanent Resident visa, also known as the "juke," is issued to foreign nationals who wish to live in Japan indefinitely. Holders of this visa can stay in Japan indefinitely and engage in any work or activity. Applicants must meet several requirements and eligibility criteria to qualify for this visa.

Firstly, applicants must have lived in Japan for at least ten years. However, for those who have been married to a Japanese national or permanent resident for at least three years and have lived in Japan for at least one year, the requirement is reduced to 5 years. Additionally, applicants must hold a valid residence status in Japan, such as a work visa, student visa, or spouse visa.

Financial stability is also a crucial factor in the application process. Applicants must have a stable source of income and sufficient savings or assets to support themselves and their families in Japan. Tax compliance is also essential, and applicants must have paid all taxes owed to the Japanese government.

Furthermore, applicants must have no criminal record and not engage in illegal activities. They must have made significant contributions to Japanese society, such as continual work history, volunteer activities, or other forms of community involvement. Applicants must also have sufficient Japanese language proficiency to live and work in Japan.

It is important to note that meeting these requirements does not guarantee approval of the Permanent Resident visa. The final decision is at the discretion of the Japanese government, and applicants may be required to provide additional documentation or attend an interview as part of the application process.

Each visa type has its own requirements and limitations, and the application process can be complex. It is essential for foreigners to carefully review the conditions and seek guidance from a qualified immigration lawyer or consultant before applying for a visa in Japan.

Chapter Four: Land Your Dream Job in Japan, The Ultimate Guide for International Job Seekers

Job Research:

For a foreigner looking to work in Japan, researching companies and industries is essential in the job search process. This is particularly important for those who need to become more familiar with the Japanese job market, culture, and business practices. By conducting thorough research, job seekers can better understand the types of companies and industries that may be a good fit for them and can also prepare themselves for job interviews.

Firstly, researching companies and industries can help job seekers identify potential employers that align with their career goals, values, and interests. Understanding the company's mission, values, and work culture is essential to determine if it is a good fit. For example, some companies in Japan may prioritize work-life balance or offer extensive employee training programs. Others may have a hierarchical management structure or expect employees to work long hours. Knowing this information beforehand can help job seekers decide which companies to target.

Secondly, it can also help job seekers prepare for job interviews. In Japan, it is common for interviewers to ask detailed questions about the company and industry during the interview process. This can include questions about the company's history, products or services, competitors, and industry trends. By conducting research beforehand, job seekers can prepare thoughtful answers and demonstrate their interest and knowledge during the interview.

Researching the Japanese job market and industries can also help job seekers understand the current job market trends and demand. For instance, some industries may be experiencing a high demand for specific skill sets, while others may face a shortage of qualified candidates. This knowledge can help job seekers decide which industries to target and which skills to develop or improve.

This can also help job seekers identify potential networking opportunities. In Japan, networking and personal connections are highly valued, and many job opportunities are found through personal referrals. By researching companies and industries, job seekers can identify key industry events, conferences, or meetups to help them expand their professional network and connect with potential employers.

Researching companies and industries can help job seekers identify potential employers that align with their career goals, values, and interests, prepare for job interviews, understand the current job market trends and demand, and identify potential networking opportunities. By investing time and effort into research, job seekers can increase their chances of finding a job that is a good fit for them and achieving their career goals in Japan.

Job Resume/CV:

One of the most critical aspects of job searching in Japan is tailoring your resume and cover letter to the job and company you are applying to. Customizing your application materials to match the job requirements and using keywords and phrases that match the job description is essential. In Japan, resumes usually follow a strict format. The most common design is the "rirekisho," a Japanese-style resume form that lists your personal information, educational background, work experience, and other qualifications in a specific order.

When creating a resume for jobs in Japan, following these guidelines and paying attention to details is essential. One crucial aspect is language proficiency, as Japanese is the official language of Japan. A well-written and well-translated Japanese-language resume can demonstrate your commitment to understanding and working in Japanese culture, even if the job doesn't require Japanese language skills. The top of your resume should include your name, address, phone number, and email address. It's also common to have a passport-style photo, though it's not required.

Your educational background should be in reverse chronological order, starting with your most recent degree or certification. Include the institution's name, major, degree or certificate earned, and any relevant coursework. Work experience should also be listed chronologically, starting with your most recent job. Include the company's name, job title, employment dates, and a brief description of your responsibilities and accomplishments. If you need more work experience, include any relevant internships or volunteer work.

Skills and qualifications should be listed separately and include any relevant abilities, such as language proficiency, computer skills, certifications, or other capabilities not covered in your educational or work experience sections. Include any additional information relevant to the job you're applying for, such as publications, awards, or professional affiliations.

It's essential to thoroughly proofread your resume for any grammatical errors or typos. It's also a good idea to have a native Japanese speaker review your resume to ensure it is culturally appropriate and well-written. Researching the company and position is crucial when applying for jobs in Japan, and you should include any relevant skills or experience that make you a strong fit for the job. Following these guidelines and tailoring your resume to the job can increase your chances of landing a job in Japan.

Where to Apply for Jobs:

GaijinPot Jobs (https://jobs.gaijinpot.com/): One of the most popular job boards for foreigners in Japan. Offers a variety of job listings, including teaching, engineering, IT, and hospitality.

Daijob.com (https://www.daijob.com/): A job board focused on Japan's mid-to-high-level positions. Offers a range of jobs across various industries, including finance, IT, engineering, and consulting.

CareerCross (https://www.careercross.com/): A job board with a strong focus on bilingual professionals. It offers various jobs across various industries, including IT, finance, marketing, and hospitality.

Japan Times Jobs (https://jobs.japantimes.com/): Job board affiliated with the Japan Times newspaper. It offers various jobs across various industries, including teaching, IT, finance, and hospitality.

JREC-IN (https://jrecin.jst.go.jp/seek/SeekTop?ln=en): A job board focused on academic and research positions in Japan. Offers a range of jobs across various academic fields, including engineering, sciences, humanities, and social sciences.

Jobs in Japan (https://jobsinjapan.com/): A job board focusing on teaching and hospitality jobs in Japan. Offers a range of job listings across various cities in Japan.

CareerEngine (https://careerengine.org/): A job board focusing on IT and engineering jobs in Japan. Offers a range of job listings across various industries, including automotive, electronics, and software.

Interview Preparation:

Preparing for a job interview in Japan can be daunting, especially for foreigners who may need to become more familiar with Japanese employers' cultural norms and expectations. If you are selected for an interview, you must prepare thoroughly by researching the company, practicing common interview questions, and learning about Japanese business culture and etiquette.

Before the interview, it's essential to research the company and the industry better to understand its values, mission, and current projects. This will help you tailor your answers to the company's needs and show that you have done your homework. Additionally, while it is only sometimes required to be fluent in Japanese for every job in Japan, having at least basic proficiency in the language will show that you are serious about working in Japan and have tried to learn it. Practice your Japanese language skills beforehand to feel more confident during the interview.

In Japan, it's important to dress professionally for job interviews. Conservative business attire is recommended, such as a suit and tie for men and a business dress or suit for women. Furthermore, job interviews in Japan may differ from what you are used to in your home country. The interview format may include a written test, a group interview, or even a social dinner with the company's executives. Make sure you understand the structure beforehand and prepare accordingly.

Showing respect and humility is highly valued in Japan. Use polite language and bow to show respect to the interviewer during the interview. Also, avoid being overly confident or boastful about your achievements and instead focus on demonstrating your willingness to learn and grow. There are also common interview questions you can expect to be asked in Japan, such as about your strengths and weaknesses, previous work experience, and why you want to work for the company. Prepare your answers beforehand to feel more confident during the interview.

After the interview, send a thank-you email to the interviewer to express your gratitude for the opportunity to interview for the position. This will show that you are courteous and interested in the position. Preparing for a job interview in Japan requires research, language skills, and cultural awareness. By following these steps, foreigners can feel more confident and prepared for the interview process in Japan.

Hiring a Recruiter:

When finding employment opportunities in Japan, hiring a recruiting firm can be an intelligent move for foreign job seekers. Recruiting firms offer various services to help job seekers navigate the hiring process and find opportunities that align with their skills and career goals.

One of the primary benefits of using a recruiting firm is access to a network of employers. These firms typically have established relationships with various companies across different industries, which means they can connect job seekers with potential employers matching their qualifications and experience. A recruiting firm can be beneficial for foreigners who may have a weak network in Japan or need to become more familiar with the local job market.

Recruiting firms can also assist with job search activities. They can offer guidance on how to write a strong resume and cover letter, prepare for interviews, and even provide career counseling. These services can be beneficial for foreigners who may be unfamiliar with Japanese hiring practices, cultural norms, and salary expectations.

Another advantage of using a recruiting firm is its specialized expertise. Many recruiting firms specialize in specific industries or job functions. This means they have a deep understanding of the skills and experience required for particular roles, as well as the industry's trends and challenges. This can be invaluable for job seekers seeking specialized roles or having niche skills.

Finally, recruiting firms can provide support throughout the entire hiring process. They can offer feedback on job applications, help negotiate salary and benefits, and even follow up with employers after interviews. This level of support can be particularly beneficial for foreign job seekers who may need to become more familiar with the nuances of the hiring process in Japan.

Of course, choosing the right recruiting firm for your needs is essential. You should research and look for a firm with a good reputation and a track record of success. Choosing a firm that specializes in your industry or job function and has experience working with foreigners is also essential. Remember that recruiting firms typically charge a fee for their services, which can vary based on the firm and the services provided.

Hiring a recruiting firm can be an intelligent investment for foreign job seekers looking to work in Japan. By leveraging these firms' expertise, network, and resources, job seekers can increase their chances of finding meaningful employment in Japan.

Patience and Persistence:

Being patient and persistent is essential when job hunting and interviewing, especially for foreigners looking to work in Japan. One reason for this is that the job market in Japan can be competitive, with a highly educated and skilled workforce. This means that it may take longer to find a job and require more persistence and patience. Additionally, the hiring process in Japan can be lengthy, with multiple rounds of interviews and assessments. This can make it take longer to hear from employers and secure a job offer.

Foreigners may also face language and cultural barriers when job hunting and interviewing in Japan. This can make it more challenging to communicate effectively with employers and to understand the expectations of the local job market. Moreover, building relationships takes time in Japan, which is vital for personal and professional success. This means that job seekers may need to establish connections with potential employers and build the trust necessary to secure a job offer.

Despite these challenges, patience and persistence can pay off in the long run. Job seekers can maintain their motivation and perseverance by setting realistic goals, breaking them down into smaller, manageable steps, and staying organized by keeping track of job applications, interviews, and follow-up activities. Seeking support from friends, family, and professionals can also be helpful. Staying positive and maintaining a positive attitude during the job search process is essential. Celebrating small successes and reminding oneself of their strengths and accomplishments can help.

In conclusion, being patient and persistent is crucial when job hunting and going through the interview process in Japan. It may take longer to find a job and navigate the hiring process, but with the right mindset and strategies, job seekers can increase their chances of finding meaningful employment in Japan.

Chapter Five: Mastering the Cultural Edge for Navigating the Interview Process in Japan as a Foreigner

Pay Attention to Your Appearance:

In Japan, paying attention to your appearance is an essential aspect of job interviews, and it significantly impacts the interview outcome. In Japanese culture, a high value is placed on appearances and first impressions, which extends to the job interview process. Making a positive first impression is vital because it can influence the interviewer's perception of your professionalism, competence, and suitability for the role. As a result, dressing appropriately and presenting yourself well can increase your chances of success.

Dressing appropriately for a job interview is also a sign of respect for the interviewer and the company. It shows that you take the interview seriously and are willing to put effort into making a good impression. This can help build rapport with the interviewer and create a positive image of you as a candidate. By dressing well, you show that you have taken the time to prepare and understand the importance of the interview process.

In Japan, cultural norms and expectations around dress and appearance differ from other countries. For instance, Japanese business attire typically includes dark suits and conservative clothing; visible tattoos or piercings are often seen as unprofessional. Adhering to these cultural norms is crucial because it demonstrates that you understand and respect Japanese culture and are willing to adapt to local customs. Doing so can increase your chances of being perceived as a suitable candidate for the position.

Dressing appropriately for a job interview reflects your attention to detail and professionalism. Employers are looking for meticulous and detail-oriented candidates, and dressing well can indicate that you take pride in your appearance and are committed to presenting yourself in a polished and professional manner. This can give the interviewer confidence in your ability to perform well professionally.

Your appearance is an essential aspect of job interviews in Japan. By dressing appropriately and presenting yourself well, you can make a positive first impression, demonstrate respect for the interviewer and the company, adhere to cultural norms, and reflect your attention to detail and professionalism. Taking the time to prepare for your appearance can significantly increase your chances of success in the job interview process.

Learn Some Japanese Phrases:

Learning some Japanese phrases can benefit a job interview in Japan, particularly for foreigners needing to be fluent. Here are some reasons why:

Firstly, learning Japanese phrases can demonstrate your interest in and respect for the local culture. Japanese employers often value candidates who appreciate their culture and are willing to try to understand it. Using basic Japanese phrases such as "hello" (konnichiwa) and "thank you" (arigatou gozaimasu) can show that you are respectful and interested in Japanese customs.

Secondly, using Japanese phrases can help establish rapport and build trust with the interviewer. Building relationships and establishing trust are critical aspects of business interactions in Japan. Using a few Japanese phrases can help break the ice and create a positive impression, which can help build rapport with the interviewer and increase your chances of success.

Thirdly, using Japanese phrases can help you navigate the interview process more smoothly. While many Japanese employers may speak English, there may be miscommunication or misunderstandings due to language differences. Using a few Japanese phrases can help clarify any confusion and ensure that you and the interviewer are on the same page.

Learning some Japanese phrases can help you stand out from other candidates. While it may not be necessary to be fluent in Japanese for many jobs, showing that you have tried to learn some basic phrases can set you apart from other candidates and demonstrate your dedication to the job and the company.

Learning some Japanese phrases can be a valuable asset in a job interview in Japan. It can show your respect and interest in the local culture, help establish rapport and trust with the interviewer, facilitate communication, and set you apart from other candidates. Even if you are not fluent in the language, learning a few basic phrases can go a long way in making a positive impression and increasing your chances of success in the interview process.

Arrive Early:

Arriving early is an essential aspect of job interviews in Japan. In Japanese culture, punctuality is highly valued, and being late is considered disrespectful and unprofessional. Here are some reasons why arriving early is essential:

First Impressions: Arriving early for a job interview in Japan is a way to make a positive first impression. It demonstrates that you respect the interviewer's time and are committed to the interview process. This can create a positive impression of you as a candidate and may also help to put you at ease before the interview begins.

Technical Issues: Arriving early also gives you time to deal with any technical issues or unforeseen circumstances that may arise. For example, you may need to navigate an unfamiliar public transportation system or find parking near the interview location. By arriving early, you can give yourself extra time to deal with these issues and ensure you arrive at the interview on time.

Prepare Mentally: Arriving early can also give you time to prepare for the interview mentally. You should review your notes, practice responding to potential questions, or take a few deep breaths to calm your nerves. By arriving early, you can do this without feeling rushed or distracted.

Show Initiative: Arriving early is also a way to demonstrate initiative and enthusiasm for the job. It shows that you are eager to make a good impression and willing to go the extra mile. This can help to set you apart from other candidates and make you a more attractive candidate for the job.

Overall, arriving early is an essential aspect of job interviews in Japan. Demonstrating punctuality, respect for the interviewer's time, and initiative can make a positive first impression and increase your chances of success.

Bring a Gift:

Bringing a gift to a job interview is an essential aspect of Japanese culture and can make a positive impression on your potential employer. Gift-giving is deeply ingrained in Japanese society and plays a vital role in building relationships. In Japan, gift-giving is a critical way to show gratitude and respect. Bringing a gift to a job interview demonstrates that you appreciate the time and effort the interviewer has taken to meet with you and are grateful for the opportunity to interview for the position. This can help build a positive relationship with the interviewer and create a good impression.

You also demonstrate your awareness of and respect for Japanese culture. Gift-giving is an essential part of Japanese etiquette, and bringing a gift to a business meeting or social occasion is customary. Following this custom shows that you understand and are willing to adapt to local customs and cultural norms. This can help you build rapport with your interviewer and show that you are a thoughtful and respectful candidate.

It shows that you pay attention to detail and are well-prepared. Choosing an appropriate gift takes time and effort, demonstrating your commitment to making a good impression and your attention to detail. By selecting a thoughtful and right gift, you can show that you are a meticulous and detail-oriented candidate who takes the interview process seriously.

When choosing a gift for a job interview, it's essential to consider the type of gift and its appropriateness for the situation. Typical gifts include small items such as high-quality stationery, sweets, or souvenirs from your hometown. It's crucial to avoid too personal or extravagant gifts, as this may be seen as inappropriate or excessive. When presenting the gift, it's essential to do so with the proper timing and etiquette. In Japan, gifts are typically given at the end of the interview, and expressing your gratitude and appreciation is important. It's also essential to present the gift thoughtfully and respectfully, such as in a nicely wrapped package or a small bag with a bow.

This is an essential aspect of Japanese culture and can make a positive impression on your potential employer. It demonstrates gratitude and respect, reflects cultural awareness, and shows attention to detail. When choosing a gift, it's essential to consider the appropriateness of the gift, timing, and presentation and avoid too personal or extravagant gifts. Following these guidelines can make a positive impression and show your potential employer that you understand and respect Japanese customs and cultural norms.

Be Humble and Respectful:

Being humble and respectful is an essential aspect of Japanese culture, and it is imperative in the context of a job interview. This cultural value is deeply ingrained in Japanese society, and understanding it is critical for those seeking employment in Japan. When interviewing for a job, showing respect to the interviewer and the company is essential. This can be demonstrated through your tone of voice, body language, and choice of words. Candidates who demonstrate a humble and respectful attitude are viewed more positively in Japan.

One reason for the importance of humility and respect in a job interview is the respect for authority ingrained in Japanese culture. In Japan, authority figures are highly respected, extending to the job interview process. It is essential to show respect to the interviewer, who represents the company and demonstrate your willingness to learn from them. This is a way to show your potential employer that you understand the importance of hierarchy and are willing to operate within it.

Another reason why humility is essential in a job interview is to avoid coming across as arrogant. In Japan, modesty is highly valued, and candidates who appear boastful or self-promoting are often viewed negatively. By demonstrating humility, you can show that you are a team player and are willing to work collaboratively with others. This attitude is valued in Japan, where teamwork is highly valued, and collaboration is critical for success.

In addition to avoiding arrogance, demonstrating a humble and respectful attitude can show your potential employer that you are willing to learn and adapt. In Japan, there is a strong emphasis on continuous learning and improvement, and candidates willing to learn and take on new challenges are often highly valued. A humble and respectful attitude can demonstrate to your potential employer that you are open-minded and ready to embrace new ideas and work methods.

Trust is a critical aspect of Japanese business culture, and it is crucial to demonstrate that you are reliable and can be trusted to fulfill your duties and responsibilities. A humble and respectful attitude can go a long way in building trust with your potential employer, and this can increase your chances of success in the job interview process.

It is an essential aspect of job interviews in Japan. It shows respect for authority, avoids arrogance, demonstrates a willingness to learn, and builds trust with your potential employer. By establishing these qualities, you can make a positive impression and increase your chances of success in the job interview process.

Practice Proper Body Language:

Practicing proper body language is an essential component of job interviews in Japan. The culture places a high value on nonverbal communication, which can significantly impact your impression of your potential employer. Demonstrating respect is crucial, and proper body language can help convey this. In Japan, bowing is a common way to show respect, and knowing the appropriate depth and duration of the bow for different situations is vital. Eye contact is also critical, showing you are attentive and engaged.

Proper body language can also show that you are confident and self-assured. In Japan, posture and facial expressions are essential indicators of confidence. Sitting up straight, maintaining eye contact, and avoiding fidgeting can all help convey a sense of confidence and professionalism. Conversely, poor posture, avoiding eye contact, or excessive fidgeting can make you appear nervous or uncertain.

Avoiding misunderstandings is another critical reason to practice proper body language. In Japan, nonverbal communication has many subtle nuances, and misinterpretation can occur if you need to become more familiar with the cultural context. For example, pointing with your finger can be seen as rude or aggressive, while nodding your head can be interpreted as agreement even if you disagree with what is being said. By being mindful of these nuances, you can avoid misunderstandings and prevent any unintended negative impact on your interview.

Building rapport is also crucial in Japanese business culture, and proper body language can help establish a positive connection with your interviewer. You can create a relationship and establish rapport by mirroring your interviewer's body language and showing empathy and understanding. This can lead to a more favorable impression and increase your chances of success in the job interview process.

Body language is an essential component of job interviews in Japan, and it demonstrates respect, confidence, and cultural awareness while helping avoid misunderstandings and build rapport with your potential employer. Paying attention to your body language and being mindful of the cultural context can make a positive impression and increase your chances of success in the job interview process.

Research the Company and Industry:

Researching the company and the industry is essential for job interviews in Japan. In Japanese culture, preparation is highly valued, and being well-informed about the company, and the industry can significantly improve your chances of success. Demonstrating interest, understanding the company culture, preparing for the interview, and showing respect for the interviewer and the company can make a positive impression and increase your chances of success.

This shows that you are genuinely interested in the job and the company. In Japan, it is essential to demonstrate enthusiasm and passion for the job and the company, and showing that you have taken the time to research and learn about the organization can demonstrate your commitment and interest. This can set you apart from other candidates who may have needed to take the time to do their homework.

It can also give you insight into the company culture. In Japan, company culture is highly valued, and it is vital to fit in with the organization's culture. By researching the company culture, you can learn about the company's values, norms, and expectations and tailor your approach and behavior accordingly. This can help you show that you are a good fit for the organization and increase your chances of being selected.

In Japan, interviews are often highly structured and formal, and understanding the company's interview process can help you anticipate the questions and prepare your answers. Additionally, researching the industry can give you insight into the company's competitors and challenges, which can help you speak intelligently about the industry and its position. This can demonstrate your knowledge and expertise in the field and increase your credibility as a candidate.

Respect for authority and seniority is highly valued, and showing that you have taken the time to learn about the organization can demonstrate your respect and appreciation for the opportunity. This can help you build rapport with the interviewer and create a positive impression.

It demonstrates interest, understanding of company culture, preparation for the interview, and respect for the interviewer and the company. By taking the time to research and learn about the organization, you can increase your chances of success in the job interview process and ultimately land your dream job.

Chapter Six: Unlocking Japan with A Step-by-Step Guide to Securing Your Visa

Preparation steps:

Preparing for a work visa in Japan requires significant time and effort, but following the proper steps and having all the necessary documents can lead to a successful application process. To obtain a work visa, the applicant must first receive a Certificate of Eligibility (COE) from the Japanese Immigration Bureau. Once the COE has been issued, the applicant must gather all necessary documents to submit along with their visa application. These include a valid passport, a completed visa application form, a passport-sized photo, certified copies of educational qualifications, a letter of employment from their employer in Japan, proof of financial stability, a criminal record check, and any other documents required for the specific type of visa being applied for.

It is important to note that the requirements for a work visa in Japan may vary depending on the specific type of visa being applied for, such as a professor visa or a skilled labor visa. Thus, checking the particular requirements for the visa being applied for is essential to ensure that all necessary documents are included in the application. Additionally, all records not in Japanese must be translated by a certified translator.

After the necessary documents have been gathered and translated, the applicant must submit their visa application to the Japanese embassy or consulate in their home country. The processing time for a work visa application can vary, so applying well before the intended start date of employment in Japan is recommended. It is also essential to work closely with an employer or sponsor in Japan and seek the guidance of a professional immigration lawyer or consultant to ensure a successful application process.

Overall, preparing for a work visa in Japan requires careful attention to detail and adherence to the specific requirements for the visa being applied for. By following the steps outlined above and seeking the guidance of professionals, applicants can increase their chances of success in obtaining a work visa in Japan.

Completing the Application:

When applying for a work visa in Japan, following the proper steps and ensuring all necessary documents are submitted wholly and accurately is crucial. Here is a breakdown of the process for applying for a Japanese work visa:

Step 1: Download the application form

The first step is to download the visa application form from the website of the Japanese embassy or consulate in your home country. Make sure to download the correct format for the type of visa you are applying for.

Step 2: Fill out the form

The application form will ask for your personal, passport, and employment details. It is vital to fill out the form accurately and completely. Any mistakes or omissions could lead to delays or rejection of your application.

Step 3: Provide a photo

You must attach a recent passport-size photo of yourself to the application form, and the image must have been taken within the last six months.

Step 4: Write a cover letter

Along with the application form, you must submit a cover letter explaining the purpose of your visit to Japan and why you are applying for a work visa. The cover letter should be concise, professional, and formal in Japanese or English.

Step 5: Submit supporting documents

In addition to the application form and cover letter, you will also need to submit several supporting documents, such as a valid passport, a certificate of eligibility (if required), your resume or CV, a letter of invitation from your employer in Japan, a certificate of employment or degree certificate, financial documents, and a health certificate (depending on your nationality and length of stay in Japan).

Step 6: Submit the application

Once you have completed the application form and gathered all necessary supporting documents, you can submit your application to the Japanese embassy or consulate in your home country. Remember to pay the visa application fee at the time of submission.

Step 7: Wait for a decision

The processing time for a Japanese work visa can vary depending on the embassy or consulate and the volume of applications being processed. Generally, it takes between one and four weeks to receive a decision on your visa application. If your application is approved, the embassy or consulate will affix a visa to your passport, allowing you to enter Japan and work legally.

By following these steps and ensuring that all necessary documents are submitted accurately, you can ultimately increase your chances of a successful application for a Japanese work visa.

Submitting the Documents:

Submitting a visa application form for a work visa in Japan requires several steps. The first step is to choose the Japanese embassy or consulate to process your application. This will usually be the embassy or consulate that has jurisdiction over the area where you live.

Before submitting your visa application form, you must gather all the required documents. This may include your passport, a certificate of eligibility, a letter of guarantee from your employer, proof of your qualifications and work experience, and other supporting documents relevant to your application.

Once you have gathered all the required documents, you must fill out the visa application form. This can usually be done online, although some embassies or consulates may require a paper form to be filled out. You must provide personal information, details about your planned stay in Japan, and information about your employment and qualifications.

You must also pay the visa application fee when submitting your visa application form. This fee varies depending on the type of visa you are applying for and the embassy or consulate processing your application.

After filling out the visa application form and paying the fee, you must submit your application to the Japanese embassy or consulate. This can typically be done in person or by mail, and some embassies or consulates may also allow you to submit your application online.

Once you have submitted your visa application form, you must wait for it to be processed. Processing times can vary depending on the embassy or consulate and the volume of applications they receive. You may also be required to attend an interview or provide additional documentation before your application is approved.

If your visa application is approved, you will receive your visa. This will typically be affixed to your passport, and you can enter Japan and begin working. You will know why if your application is denied and can appeal the decision.

Things to Avoid:

When applying for a visa to Japan, it is crucial to take steps to ensure that your application is complete, accurate, and meets all the eligibility requirements. There are several potential pitfalls that applicants may encounter, and one common mistake is submitting incomplete or incorrect documentation, which can delay or reject the application. It is crucial to carefully read the requirements for your specific visa type and provide all the necessary documents.

Another area for improvement is applying early enough. Some visas can take several weeks or even months to process, so checking the processing times for your specific visa type and planning accordingly is essential. Applying too late can result in your visa not being processed for your planned travel dates.

It is essential to be honest, and accurate when filling out your application and to provide any additional information or documentation that may be required. Providing false or misleading information on a visa application can lead to severe consequences, including being banned from entering Japan. Additionally, not meeting eligibility requirements or failing to follow visa regulations can result in your application being rejected, fines, deportation, or other legal consequences.

Overstaying your visa can also lead to severe consequences, including being banned from entering Japan in the future. Be sure to carefully monitor the expiration date of your visa and make arrangements to extend or renew it if necessary. If you plan to stay in Japan for an extended period, apply for a long-term visa to stay in the country legally.

Changing from a tourist visa to a work visa in Japan is generally not recommended. This is because engaging in work activities while in Japan on a tourist visa is illegal. Suppose you are caught violating immigration laws by engaging in work activities on a tourist visa. In that case, you can be deported and barred from entering Japan for a certain period. Additionally, applying for a work visa while in Japan on a tourist visa may make it easier to obtain a work visa.

In summary, to avoid potential pitfalls when applying for a visa to Japan, it is essential to carefully read the requirements for your specific visa type, provide all necessary documentation, and comply with all regulations associated with your visa type. If you have any questions or concerns about the visa application process, it may be helpful to consult with a professional immigration lawyer or consultant.

PART III: Conclusion

The process can be complex and time-consuming when it comes to obtaining a visa for Japan. It is essential to take the time to read and understand the specific requirements for your visa type and provide all necessary documentation. Please do so to avoid delays or even rejection of your application. Some common pitfalls to be aware of include submitting incomplete or incorrect documentation, not applying early enough, providing false information, not meeting eligibility requirements, failing to follow visa regulations, and overstaying your visa. It is also important to note that changing from a tourist visa to a work visa in Japan is generally not recommended, as this can have serious consequences.

In Japan, job interviews differ from what you may be used to in other countries. To increase your chances of success, it is vital to research the company, the position you are applying for, and the Japanese business culture. This can include learning about the company's values and mission, their approach to work, and team dynamics. In the interview, you can be asked about your background and experience, your motivation for applying to the company, and how you would handle certain work-related situations. It is also important to dress professionally and arrive early to the interview.

Japanese business culture can differ significantly from what you may be used to in Western countries. To work successfully in Japan, it is crucial to be aware of these differences and to adapt your behavior accordingly. Some key differences include the importance of hierarchy and respect for authority, the emphasis on group harmony and consensus-building, and the importance of indirect communication. It is also essential to understand the concept of "honne" and "tatemae," which refer to the difference between a person's true thoughts and feelings and what they express in public.

While working in Japan without speaking Japanese is possible, having basic language knowledge can be extremely helpful. Not only can it improve communication with coworkers and clients, but it can also demonstrate a willingness to learn and integrate into the culture. Additionally, potential employers can view learning Japanese positively, as it shows a dedication to the job and a willingness to adapt.

Working in Japan can be a rewarding and fulfilling experience, but it is essential to be aware of the cultural differences and potential challenges that may arise. By carefully preparing for a job interview, understanding Japanese business culture, and obtaining a Japanese visa, you can increase your chances of success in a Japanese work environment. Additionally, taking the time to learn the Japanese language can improve your communication skills and demonstrate a willingness to learn and adapt to the culture. By being aware of and respecting Japanese culture and customs, you can thrive in a Japanese work environment and build positive relationships with colleagues and clients.

Relevant Materials:

It's important to note that visa application fees and requirements are subject to change without prior notice. As such, it's recommended that you check with your nearest Japanese embassy or consulate for the latest information before applying for a visa. The fees for Japanese visas can vary depending on the type of visa and the country where the application is made. Therefore, obtaining the most up-to-date information from the relevant embassy or consulate is crucial before beginning the application process. Please do so to avoid delays or even the rejection of your visa application.

United States visas and costs for references (March 2023)

Work visa:	40 USD
Student visa:	120 USD
Dependent visa:	120 USD
Technical intern visa:	50 USD
Spouse visa:	120 USD
Working holiday visa:	41 USD
Cultural activities visa:	40 USD
Permanent Resident visa:	100 USD

United Kingdom visas and costs for references (2021)

Work visa:	250 GBP

Student visa:	170 GBP
Dependent visa:	170 GBP
Technical intern visa:	25 GBP
Spouse visa:	No Fee
Working holiday visa:	58 GBP
Cultural activities visa:	70 GBP
Permanent Resident visa:	170 GBP

Canada visas and costs for references (2021)

Work visa:	125 CAD
Student visa:	exempted
Dependent visa:	85 CAD
Technical intern visa:	85 CAD
Working holiday visa:	58 CAD
Cultural activities visa:	70 CAD
Permanent Resident visa:	1120 CAD
Trainee visa:	+85 CAD

Australia visas and costs for references (2021)

Work visa:	120 AUD
Student visa:	125 AUD
Dependent visa:	80 AUD
Technical intern visa:	40 AUD
Permanent Resident visa:	360 AUD
Trainee visa:	80 AUD

New Zealand visas and costs for references (2021)

Work visa:	95 NZD
Student visa:	270 NZD
Dependent visa:	40 NZD
Technical intern visa:	50 NZD
Permanent Resident visa:	105 NZD

About the Author

Brian Takahashi is an American living and working in Japan for over a decade. During his time in Japan, he has worked in various industries, including management, tourism, and education, and has applied for different types of visas to continue his employment. With his extensive experience in the Japanese work environment, he has gained a deep understanding of the cultural differences and challenges of working in Japan.

Brian is also married to a Japanese woman with two children. His personal experiences have given him a unique perspective on Japanese culture and family life, which he has shared with others through his writing and speaking engagements.

As a bilingual speaker of English and Japanese, Brian has bridged the communication gap between Japanese and non-Japanese coworkers and clients. He has also used his language skills to volunteer as a translator for various community events and organizations.

Brian's passion for Japan and its culture has led him to become a respected member of the ex-pat community in Japan. His insights and knowledge about life and work in Japan have been valuable to those considering living or working there.

www.ingramcontent.com/pod-product-compliance
Lightning Source LLC
Chambersburg PA
CBHW070318240526
45467CB00046B/1933